ALSO BY JUDITH VIORST

POEMS

The Village Square
It's Hard to Be Hip Over Thirty and Other Tragedies of Married Life
People and Other Aggravations
How Did I Get to Be Forty and Other Atrocities
If I Were in Charge of the World and Other Worries
When Did I Stop Being Twenty and Other Injustices
Forever Fifty and Other Negotiations
Sad Underwear and Other Complications

CHILDREN'S BOOKS

Sunday Morning
I'll Fix Anthony
Try It Again, Sam
The Tenth Good Thing About Barney
Alexander and the Terrible, Horrible, No Good, Very Bad Day
My Mama Says There Aren't Any Zombies, Ghosts, Vampires, Creatures,
    Demons, Monsters, Fiends, Goblins, or Things
Rosie and Michael
Alexander, Who Used to Be Rich Last Sunday
The Good-bye Book
Earrings!
The Alphabet From Z to A (With Much Confusion on the Way)
Alexander, Who's Not (Do You Hear Me? I Mean It!) Going to Move

OTHER

Yes, Married
A Visit From St. Nicholas (To a Liberated Household)
Love & Guilt & the Meaning of Life, Etc.
Necessary Losses
Murdering Mr. Monti
Imperfect Control
You're Officially a Grown-Up

Suddenly Sixty

AND OTHER SHOCKS
OF LATER LIFE

JUDITH VIORST

Illustrated by Laurie Rosenwald

Simon & Schuster
NEW YORK   LONDON   TORONTO   SYDNEY   SINGAPORE

SIMON & SCHUSTER
Rockefeller Center
1230 Avenue of the Americas
New York, NY 10020

Designed by Karolina Harris
Manufactured in the United States of America
5 7 9 10 8 6 4
Library of Congress Cataloging-in-Publication Data
Viorst, Judith.
Suddenly sixty and other shocks of later life / Judith Viorst; illustrated by Laurie Rosenwald.
p. cm.
1. Humorous poetry, American. 2. Aging—Poetry. 3. Women—Poetry.
I. Title: Suddenly 60 and other shocks of later life. II. Title.
PS3572.I6 S8 2000   811'.54—dc21   00-033847
ISBN 0-684-86763-X

For Jan Jaffe Kahn
and Linda Ehren Keninger

Contents

THE CHILDREN AND GRANDCHILDREN

OTHER SHOCKS

Suddenly Sixty

It's Harder to Be Frisky Over Sixty

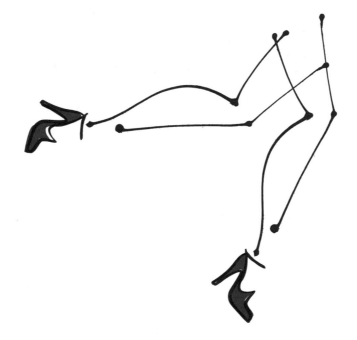

Inside my shoes and my panty hose
I've painted blue nail polish on my toes,
A skirmish in the war that I wage
Against the constraints of my current age.
Despite the advent of Medicare,
I will still buy bikini underwear
And scorn the notion that seniorhood
Means it's too late to be up to no good.

I would if I could.

Don't give me extra time to walk down the jetway.
And please don't get up and give me your seat on the bus.
I'd rather be engagée than Emeritus,
Though it's harder to be frisky over sixty.

I'm not prepared to sign up for Elderhostel.
Retirement communities? Save your brochures.
I'll keep right on trucking as long as my strength endures,
Though it's harder to be frisky over sixty.

I'm standing firm against the Early Bird Special.
I'm out on the dance floor strutting what's left of my stuff.
I'd rather say never say die than enough is enough,
Though it's harder to be frisky over sixty.

I don't intend to stop showing a little cleavage.
Nor do I intend to stop flashing a little thigh.
I'm still not too old to give it the old college try,
Though it's harder to keep trying,
And it's harder to keep trucking,
And it's harder to be frisky over sixty.

THE BLISSFUL COUPLE

They laugh together.
Read together.
Dance together.
Paint together.
Listen to music together.
Walk, holding hands, together.

They love exchanging
Warm
Wet
Mushy
Kisses.

He rushes to greet her,
His arms outstretched,
Joyfully calling her name,
When he sees her arrive.

Who, you are wondering,
Is this blissful couple?
She is his grandma.
He is almost five.

A's for arthritis.
B's for bad back.
C is for chest pains. Corned beef? Cardiac?
D is for dental decay and decline.
E is for eyesight—can't read that top line.
F is for fissures and fluid retention.
G is for gas (which I'd rather not mention)
And other such gastrointestinal glitches.
H is high blood pressure.
I is for itches.
J is for joints that are failing to flex.
L's for libido—what's happened to sex?
Wait! I forgot about K for bad knee.
(I've got a few gaps in my M—memory.)
N's for nerve (pinched) and neck (stiff) and neurosis.
O is for osteo-.
P's for -porosis.
Q is for queasiness. Fatal? Just flu?
R is for reflux—one meal becomes two.
S is for sleepless nights counting my fears.
T is for tinnitus—bells in my ears.
U is for difficulties urinary.
V is for vertigo.
W's worry
About what the X—as in X ray—will find.
But though the word "terminal" rushes to mind,
I'm proud, as each Y—year—goes by, to reveal
A reservoir of undiminished Z—zeal—
For checking the symptoms my body's deployed,
And keeping my twenty-six doctors employed.

OLD FRIENDS

Old friends. We are very old friends, as in
We've known each other so long
We knew each other back when we were virgins,
Back when we helped each other figure out how far to go,
And whether we ought to go there, and with whom,
Back when we experimented with hating our parents and loving
    de Beauvoir and Sartre,
Back when we talked, with the same degree of passionate intensity,
About eyeliner and the meaning of the universe.

Old friends, grown up and still friends. We exchanged
Our recipes for meat loaf and for marriage,
And our remedies for when we messed them up,
Assuring each other, over the phone calls or coffee,
That though we had screamed at our children we were basically
    decent mothers,
And that though we had gained seven pounds we were basically
    slim,
And that though, at this moment, we most sincerely wished to kill
    our husbands, we basically didn't.

And we talked, between the trips to the zoo and picketing the
    White House,
About eyeliner and the meaning of the universe.

Old friends, no-longer-young friends, we held hands
Through the midlife crisis, the dark night of the soul,
The jawline dividing, like Gaul, into three separate parts,
While we kept reminding each other that feeling depressed could
    be a major growth opportunity,
While we kept consulting each other on whether we needed a
    lover, or face-lift, or master's degree,
While we kept on asking each other whether this was as good
    as it gets,
And was that good enough?
While we talked, as time speeded up and our metabolism
    slowed down,
About eyeliner and the meaning of the universe.

Old friends, now almost-old friends. And at last
We see what our mothers meant
When they boringly said, As long as you have your health,
Comforting each other when we dealt with diminishing hair in our
    most private places,
Competing with each other when we bragged of our grand-
    children's brains and beauty and charm,
Crying with each other in the doctor's office when he broke
    the news.

How am I going to walk in this world without talking to my
    friend
About eyeliner and the meaning of the universe?

NOW I LAY ME DOWN TO SLEEP

If the mattress is hard, but not excessively hard,
If the comforter isn't too heavy or too light,
If the bottom sheet has been tucked in really tight,
If the temperature in the room isn't hot or freezing,
If the neighbor's cat isn't mating in the front yard,
If the neighbor's kid isn't playing acoustic guitar,
If the car alarm doesn't go off in the neighbor's car,
If my husband is neither grinding his teeth nor wheezing,
If the blackout curtains are keeping the bedroom dim,
If I don't get a cramp in my leg or a sinus attack,
If I manage to push my ten thousand anxieties back,
If I don't think I hear a burglar quietly creeping,
If two-thirds of the bed isn't occupied by him,
If at four in the morning the telephone doesn't ring,
If the *Times* is delivered gently, and no birds sing,
I might—I just actually might—do a little sleeping.

A MODEST PROPOSAL

A shrewd friend of mine is persuaded
We'd help everybody in need
If we were assured we would lose a pound
Each time we performed a good deed.

How swiftly we'd rush to contribute,
How eagerly we'd volunteer,
If giving to others could guarantee
That our waistlines would reappear.

We'd eat, without fear of reprisals,
The foods our scales used to forbid,
Knowing the flab would dissolve from our hips
As soon as we tutored a kid,

Or worked to save owls, whales, or forests,
Or read to the sick or the blind.
Spurred by the motto "The larger the heart,
The smaller will be the behind,"

We'd raise funds to shelter the homeless,
Or cure some disease, or stop war.
Seeing our silhouettes narrowing down,
We'd yearn to do more, and still more,

Delighted to make the world better
While also achieving thin thighs.
All of us folks who've been watching our weight
Would be easy to mobilize

And turn into daily do-gooders
Released from a diet regime
And enjoying a vast sense of virtuousness
Along with a lot of whipped cream.

A WHOLE OTHER STAGE

I've reached the stage where my lawyer, my broker, my allergist,
and my president are all significantly younger than I.
I've reached the stage where I recognize, when I'm buying new
living-room drapes or a new set of dishes, that they're likely to
be the last ones that I'll ever buy.
And when I'm starting to tell my friends some really terrific story,
and I ask them whether I've told them this story before, and no
matter what story I've started to tell, they say yes,
I know that I have reached a whole other stage.

I've reached the stage where I find that most of the spaces I used to
   park in are now too small for my car.
I've reached the stage where I'm no longer able to call myself
   middle-aged because that's what my children are.
And when going to see two movies at two separate theaters on the
   same day, followed by eating a sausage-and-anchovy pizza, is
   what I'm defining as orgiastic excess,
I know that I have reached a whole other stage.

I've reached the stage where a lot of the reading I'm doing is at
   the market checking salt-free and fat-free and expiration dates.
I've reached the stage where nobody bothers to look at my driver's
   license when I want to purchase tickets at senior rates.
And when I'm out of town and I phone my husband at six A.M.,
   and I ring and ring but he doesn't answer the phone, and my
   first thought is not infidelity but cardiac arrest,
I know that I have reached a whole other stage.

I've reached the stage where the people with whom I once
   discussed Marcel Proust are discussing inheritance taxes and
   living wills.
I've reached the stage where I couldn't leave my house for
   twenty-four hours unaccompanied by eight different kinds
   of pills.
And when I have to admit that, offered the choice, I'd—
   unhesitatingly—give up a night of wild rapture with Denzel
   Washington for a nice report on my next bone density test,
I know that I have reached a whole other stage.

A Brief History
of Marriage

Though it's hard to believe, we believe
We belong together.
Something has happened to suddenly make us complete.
Like Ginger and Fred we believe
We belong together.
Two separate people dancing to one single beat.

I like his good mind. And he's kind.
We belong together.
We're finding it easy to squeeze and to please and to blend.
Like Nora and Nick we believe
We belong together.
Isn't it swell making love with your very best friend.

He admires my smile. And my style.
We belong together.
In spring we'll be ready to bring on the rings and the rice.
Like Adam and Eve we believe
We belong together.
A match made in heaven. A life lived in paradise.

A life lived—at least for a while—in paradise.

Though it's hard to believe, it is hard
To belong together.
Something that used to seem boundless is starting to shrink.
Like sloppy and neat it is hard
To belong together.
How in God's name do two people share one single sink?

All his jokes are too long. It is hard
To belong together.
We get into bed and already I'm dreading his snore.
Like surly and sweet it is hard
To belong together.
What are his jockey shorts doing in my dresser drawer?

Must he gloat when I'm wrong? It is hard
To belong together.
He says that I'm sometimes a pill, sometimes shrill. Is that nice?
Like a pair of left feet, it is hard
To belong together.
Oh, where is my Adam? What happened to paradise?

Won't someone please tell me what happened to paradise?

TO BE CONTINUED

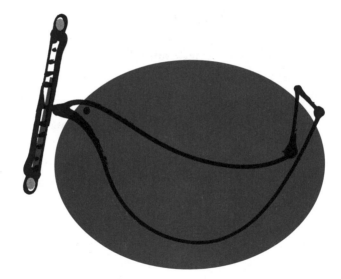

Though it's hard to belong, we believe
We belong together.
There's something between us that's stronger than all of
   the strains.
For better or worse we believe
We belong together.
And sometimes it's stardust, and sometimes it's stopped-up drains.

It's been far from ideal, yet we feel
We belong together.
In spite of the tears and tough years we've done more than
   make do.
In sickness and health we believe
We belong together.
And sometimes it's skylarks, and sometimes it's stomach flu.

Perfect match? We were wrong. Nonetheless,
We belong together.
We're counting on laughter and trust, and some lust, to suffice
Till death do us part. We believe
We belong together.
This may be the closest it gets to paradise.

And sometimes we still get a glimpse of paradise.

More on Marriage

So My Husband and I Decided to Take a Car Trip Through New England

Even if I had a Ph.D. in psychology,
Even if I were a diplomatic whiz,
Even if I were Queen of the Charmers and more irresistibly sexual
Than whoever the current reigning sexpot is,
And even if I had a fortune to squander on payoffs,
And even if I had Mafia connections,
It still would be impossible to persuade my husband, when lost,
To stop—please stop—the car, and ask for directions.

Even if I were collapsing from thirst and from hunger,
Even if I were reduced to darkest gloom,
Even if I observed, between sobs, that we should have arrived three
    hours ago,
And the inn was going to give away our room,
And even if I revived all my marital grievances:
Old hurts and humiliations and rejections,
It still would be impossible to persuade my husband, when lost,
To stop—just stop—the car, and ask for directions.

Even if I were to throw a full-scale temper tantrum,
Even if I were to call him an uncouth name,
Even if I were to not-so-gently suggest that should we wind up
    getting divorced,
He would have nobody else but himself to blame,
And even if I, in a tone I concede is called screaming,
Enumerated his countless imperfections,
It still would be impossible to persuade my husband, when lost,
To stop the goddamn car, and ask for directions.

A VERY VERY BRIEF HISTORY
OF MARRIAGE

1963—Niagara.
1999—Viagra.

IN RESPONSE TO A REQUEST FOR AN APOLOGY

*I've read that the ability to apologize is
one of the hallmarks of a mature marriage.*

I didn't say it.
I didn't do it.

You wouldn't want me to lie and accept the blame for something
    I'm not guilty of.
I believe I'm a big enough person to concede that I've been wrong
    when I've been wrong.
But I wasn't, and therefore I won't—not even for love.

I won't admit it.
I can't admit it.
I know it isn't my fault and, if it is, may God—this moment!—
    strike me down dead.
I'd gladly say I'm sorry except there's nothing for me to say I'm
    sorry *for.*
Okay, I'll take back *how* I said it, but not *what* I said.

They made me do it.
They drove me to it.
In view of all these pressures and provocations how could I have
    done otherwise?
But if you are willing to grant
That I can't be held completely responsible,
And that there are plenty of others who share the blame,
And that you're also fallible,
And that you've made mistakes,
And that, if you'd been me, you'd have done the same,
And if you are willing to promise
That you'll never throw it up to me,
And that I won't look lesser in your eyes,
Then maybe I'd be willing,
I'd probably be willing,
I guess I'm willing to
Apologize.

ANNIVERSARY DINNER

Whatever it is
That teases the palate,
Amuses the bouche,
Fizzes the champagne,
Puts the voilà in foie gras,
Sizzles the châteaubriand,
Lifts the soufflé,
And makes of this dinner
A bit of heaven on earth,
Makes you the favorite meal
Of this gourmet.

ABOUT HIS RETIREMENT

He's pointing out where I left some dust on the baseboards.
He's watching out for which foods I am letting go bad.
He's giving me guidance on how to water the houseplants.
He says that I ought to be glad. I am not glad.

He's nudging me when I fail to floss after mealtime.
He's alerting me when I gain even half a pound.
He's pestering me to straighten my spine and stop slouching
Whenever he's around. He is always around.

He's starting conversations with me when I'm reading.
He's chiming in when I talk with my friends on the phone.
He's coming with me when I shop at the supermarket
So I won't have to shop alone. I like alone.

He's sitting beside me while I'm tweezing my eyebrows.
He's standing beside me while I'm blow-drying my hair.
He's sharing those moments when I am clipping my toenails.
You want my opinion? He's overdoing share.

He's keeping track of how I am spending each second.
He also keeps track of how much I spend on my clothes.
Before he retired I told him he must find a hobby.
Now he's retired. And guess who's the hobby he chose?

A Wedding Sonnet for the Next Generation

He might compare you to a summer's day,
Declaring you're far fairer in his eyes.
She might, with depth and breadth and many sighs,
Count all the ways she loves you, way by way.

He might say when you're old and full of sleep,
He'll cherish still the Pilgrim soul in you.
She might—oh, there are poems so fine, so true,
To help you speak of love and vows to keep.

Words help. And you are writing your own poem.
It doesn't always scan or always rhyme.
It mingles images of the sublime
With plainer words: Respect. Trust. Comfort. Home.

How very rich is love's vocabulary
When friends, dear friends, best friends decide to marry.

The Children and Grandchildren

JUST A FEW WORDS OF ADVICE, JUST A FEW HELPFUL HINTS

So your son has announced that he's going to marry that woman.
You know he'll be making the biggest mistake of his life.
For a daughter-in-law even Lady Macbeth deserves better.
And even a Henry the Eighth should be spared such a wife.
So before you begin to arrange the rehearsal dinner
From cocktails to capons to chocolate-covered mints,
You intend (without being critical) to (diplomatically) offer him
Just a few words of advice, just a few helpful hints.

So your daughter is leaving a job with an excellent future.
She's pulling up roots and she's moving out West to create,
Unencumbered by furniture, money, or health insurance.
This is surely a game plan any sane person would hate.
So before she trades in her office and East Side apartment
For wind chimes, a futon, and maybe some cactus prints,
You intend (without seeming skeptical) to (quite respectfully) offer her
Just a few words of advice, just a few helpful hints.

So the parents of your new grandchild are spoiling him rotten.
He's never heard "no" or "say please" or "don't do that again."
It looks like he's worn the same shirt from last May through November.
It looks like he's going to breast-feed until he is ten.
So before his mother and father are too late to stop him
From growing up to be someone who'll make the world wince,
You intend (without sounding horrified) to (very tactfully) offer them
Just a few words of advice, just a few helpful hints.

So our daughters and sons and their spouses are no longer children.
They reach their decisions without ever calling us first.
They often unreasonably tend to look on the bright side,
While we're always asking ourselves, What if worse comes to worst?
So before they do something too fatal we will rush in with
Anything from a big hug to a check to a blintz,
In addition to which we'll continue to (oh-so-unintrusively) offer them
Just a few words of advice, just a few helpful hints.

DID I DO SOMETHING WRONG?

Quality time and vitamin C and a book before bedtime at night,
I did everything right.
Then why, when I reach out to touch him, does he hold me at bay?
Something inside of me dies
When I look in my son's shuttered eyes,
So far from here. So very far away.

Tricking and treating and soccer games and the second grade's
    Halloween show,
I was sure to go.
And yet he is stumbling through jungles of bitterest black,
Lost in the fog that he buys,
Wearing a rebel's disguise,
Unwilling, or unable, to come back.

        I never claimed to be the perfect mother.
        I made mistakes. Well, everybody did.
        But God, I was so glad to be his mother.
        And God, oh God, oh God, I loved this kid.
        I love this kid.

Patience and laughter and trips to the beach and tickles and song,
Did I do something wrong?
Am I kidding myself? Am I simply rewriting the poem?
Telling myself a few lies,
While somewhere a frightened child cries,
And I wait, and I hope, and I pray that he'll find his way home.

OUR WONDERFUL ANNUAL
FULL-FLEDGED FAMILY VACATION

It is August at the Cape,
And we're here once more
On our wonderful annual full-fledged family vacation,
Having taken (for a rent in the low five figures) a house large
  enough to accommodate
Our children, their spouses, the grandchildren, the two of us, my
  divorced sister-in-law,
And her overenthusiastic Golden Retriever,
Without whom, she made clear,
She'd rather not come.

No pets accompanied the families flown in by us
(For fares in the low five figures)
From Chicago, Jacksonville, and Austin.
And now we are here, together again for two weeks,
On our wonderful annual full-fledged family vacation,

Where I am trying, with moderate success, to overlook
The wet beach towels soaking into the living-room chairs,
The use of the kitchen table as the baby's changing table,

My sister-in-law's chartreuse thong bathing suit,
And where I am trying, with moderate success, to make pleasing meals
For the one who won't eat anything that once had a face,
For the one who won't eat anything that is green or swims,
For the one who won't eat anything unorganically grown,
For the one who won't eat anything,
And where I am trying, with moderate success, to find happy ways to
    parcel out
The car, a quart of Cherry Garcia ice cream, and my complete attention
Among adult siblings whose rivalries always return,
Unresolved, unrepressed, and untarnished by the years,
On our wonderful annual full-fledged family vacation.

I am, presumably, having a wonderful time,
Even though the organic daughter-in-law and the monthly pedicure
    daughter-in-law are not invariably en rapport
Or on speaking terms,
And even though my husband and I cannot have sex for two weeks
Because nobody knocks at our bedroom door before entering,
And even though the grandchildren and the Golden Retriever
Have done many irreparable things to our rented house,
For which there are sure to be penalties
In the low five figures.

This morning I woke up early
And, amid the smell of sweaty sneakers and bluefish,
I found myself thinking that maybe just *one* week in August,
Or maybe, now that I'm thinking such thoughts, just one weekend,
Might make for an equally wonderful,
And perhaps an even more wonderful,
Wonderful annual full-fledged family vacation.

When I watch my oldest son
With his little daughter,
Reading her books,
Or patiently braiding her hair,
Or waiting while she chooses, and changes her mind,
   and chooses, and changes her mind about
What she will wear,
And when I watch him bathing her,
Or kissing a bump on her forehead to make it better,
Or tenderly tucking her into bed at night,
I know that, though I did a lot of things wrong,
I must have done a few things right.

BEING A GRANDPARENT
IS THE BEST REVENGE

You laughed when I worried about you. Now
You have a child,
And his merest mosquito bite can cause you alarm,
But he laughs when you count the ways he could come to harm
Without your protection.

You squirmed when I snuggled with you. Now
You have a child,
And you're trying to give him a cuddle and a kiss,
But he slips from your grasp, determined to resist this
Annoying affection.

You spurned meals I made just for you. Now
You have a child,
And you've gone out and bought his favorite chicken parts,
But he tells you he's finished—one taste after he starts,
Though they're broiled to perfection.

You sighed when I said just you wait until
You have a child.
Now I'm here to assure you, unequivocably,
That though he is doing to you what you did to me,
He's not into rejection.

For he may not want your protection.
And he may not want your cuddles.
And he may not want your chicken.
But he wants mine.

THE SWEETEST OF NIGHTS AND THE FINEST OF DAYS

A SONG FOR OUR CHILDREN AND OUR CHILDREN'S CHILDREN

I wish you, I wish you,
I wish you these wishes:
Cool drinks in your glasses.
Warm food in your dishes.
People to nourish and cherish and love you.
A lamp in the window to light your way home in the haze.
I wish you the sweetest of nights
And the finest of days.

I wish you, I wish you
A talent for living.
Delight in the getting.
Delight in the giving.
A song in your soul, and someone to hear it.
The wisdom to find the right path when you're lost in a maze.
I wish you the sweetest of nights
And the finest of days.

       A snug roof above you.
       A strong self inside you.
       The courage to go where you know you must go,
       And a good heart to guide you.
       And good friends beside you.

I wish you, I wish you
A dream worth the doing.
And fortune's face smiling
On all you're pursuing.
And pleasures that far far
Outweigh your small sorrows.
Arms opened wide to embrace your tomorrows.
A long sunlit sail on the bluest and smoothest of bays.
I wish you the sweetest of nights
And the finest of days.

Other Shocks

WHEN ASKED IF I THOUGHT THAT I'D FINALLY GOT IT TOGETHER

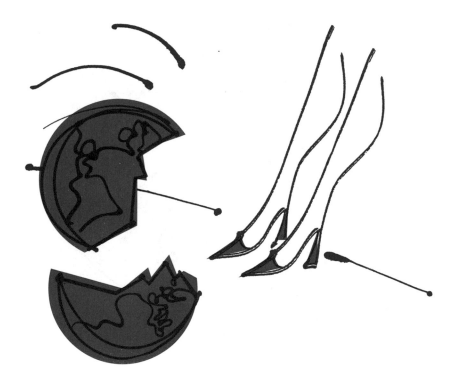

I had it together on Sunday.
By Monday at noon it had cracked.
On Tuesday debris
Was descending on me.
And by Wednesday no part was intact.
On Thursday I picked up some pieces.
On Friday I picked up the rest.
By Saturday, late,
It was almost set straight.
And on Sunday the world was impressed
With how well I had got it together.
But spare me the cheers and applause,
For as the world turns
Every sixty-plus learns
That among life's immutable laws
Is one that we're bound to be bound to
Right through to the end of our days:
That although we may get it together,
Together is not how it stays.

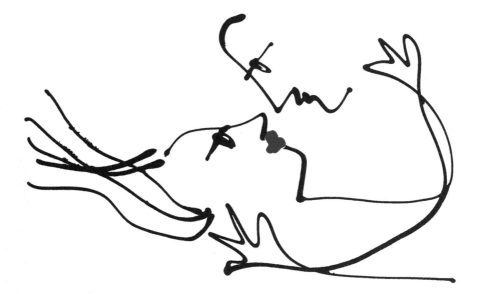

He dies.
She dies.
And after great loneliness
Those who are left behind
Find each other,
Or redefine each other

From neighbor or old friend
To companion,
Intimate,
And, most amazingly,
Lover.

Their middle-aged children
Sulk,
Saying, without saying it,
This is unseemly.
Devote yourself
To good works,
Educational cruises,
Your grandchildren,
And do not abandon
Your lost mate,
Your past life,
Or us.

Those who are left behind
Turn to each other,
Their soft used flesh
Renewed in a forgiving embrace.
And in their hearts
Such gratitude.
Such gratitude.

TO A HUSBAND WHO, AFTER FORTY-TWO YEARS, DUMPED MY WONDERFUL FRIEND FOR A MUCH YOUNGER WOMAN

May you lose your state lottery ticket the day that you win it.
May each meal that you eat leave a permanent stain on your
   clothes.
May you get unsolicited telephone calls once a minute.
May a large air-conditioning unit fall down on your toes.
May all of the hair you possess grow out of your nose.
When you zip up your pants may your zipper get stuck with you
   in it.

May you look in the mirror and shudder at what you are seeing.
May your doctor prescribe colonoscopies ten times a year.
May your high school reunion class vote you Least Loved Human
   Being.
May your chest get so droopy you need to go buy a brassiere.
May your days possess all the vibrancy of warm beer.
And throughout every night may you do far less sleeping
   than peeing.

May your license expire and you flunk the exam to renew it.
May your dirtiest deeds be exposed in the national press.
May you find yourself trying to do it much more than you
   do it.
May the answer to all of your prayers be a "no," not a "yes."
May you always be audited by the IRS.
And whenever you audit your life may you know that you
   blew it.

CEMETERIES AND OTHER PLOTS

The plan was to go on the ultimate double date,
Buy resting places for four in a charming location.
We thought of it as a very extended vacation,
For which we'd pay well in advance so as not to be late
And miss being able to pick from the widest selection
Of tombs with a view, on a hill, in the shade of a tree.
What a sensible foursome we are, although secretly
(While we've given a great deal of thought to how we would
    choose them)
None of us believe that we'll ever use them.

A THOROUGHLY MODERN SIXTY

I'm slogging along down the information highway.
I'd rather read Yeats than my computer screen,
But I'm told that I cannot survive the twenty-first century
Unless I can manage to master this machine,
Which, I have also been told, does not really hate me,
In spite of the many hostile things it does.
I aspire to being a thoroughly modern sixty,
But sometimes I don't like what is as much as what was.

I'm listening to a recorded menu of options
And suddenly my brain is turning to mush.
Do I want my prescription refilled or departures to Denver?
And when I decide this, which buttons do I push?
And why can't the calls I'm making simply be answered
By living breathing human women and men?
I aspire to being a thoroughly modern sixty,
But sometimes I don't like right now as much as back then.

I've just returned from a restful ten-day vacation.
One hour later I'm needing ten days more,
What with voice mail and E-mail and faxes demanding attention,
Plus all those FedExes delivered to my door.
Next year, I've been told, I should travel with a cell phone,
So everyone can reach me faster than fast.
I aspire to being a thoroughly modern sixty,
But sometimes I don't like the present as much as the past.

In order to be a thoroughly modern sixty
I'll learn to embrace the new technology
By conversing with virtual rather than actual people
And reordering pills by pressing button three.
I'll never leave home without my modem and pager,
Remaining in touch with all who so desire.
I aspire to being a thoroughly modern sixty,
But sometimes I don't like the sixty to which I aspire.

MORTAL QUESTION

I didn't know I wasn't there.
I will not know I'm not.
Between these two oblivions
My life unfolds its plot.

I missed the glory that was Greece.
I missed Rome's rise and fall.
My absence from these grand events
Disturbed me not at all.

Nor did I feel deprived because
They held the Renaissance
Some centuries before my birth.
No pre-existence wants

Imposed themselves upon my peace.
Why does some future spring
Collapse my heart with longing when
I will not feel a thing?

JUST LUCKY I GUESS

*I've been noticing lately that when I complain
about something bad that has happened to me,
the person to whom I'm complaining tells me
how fortunate I am that it wasn't much worse.*

When my plane lost two engines and had to go back to the airport,
They said I was lucky the plane hadn't crashed and burned.
When a mugger, at gunpoint, took both of my rings and my wallet,
They said I was lucky my credit cards were returned.
And when lightning demolished our tree, which fell on our house
and then plunged through our roof and into our bedroom,
They said I was lucky I wasn't home at the time.
Why does this happen to me? I'm
Just lucky I guess.

When my luggage was lost for three days on our trip to Bermuda,
They said I was lucky it wasn't a dress-up trip.
When I slipped on an ice patch and broke my right foot in two places,
They said I was lucky I hadn't broken my hip.
And when my cousin, the klutz, somehow managed to spill
    an entire carafe of Merlot on my carpet,
They said I was lucky my sofa escaped the spray.
Why does this happen to me? Hey,
Just lucky I guess.

When the caterer canceled and forty were coming for dinner,
They said I was lucky I'd saved the catering fee.
When I looked at the glass and I saw that the glass was half empty,
They said I was lucky I still was able to see.
And when my least favorite aunt became ill while visiting me
    this past March, and stayed on till September,
They said I was lucky she left before the next snow.
Why does this happen to me? Oh,
Just lucky I guess.

When somebody smashes my Chevy but leaves me unmangled,
I know that I ought to be grateful rather than curse.
When my endodontist performs root canal on my molars,
I know that I must keep in mind that it could have been worse.
And I know I should thank my good fortune, when disease or
    disaster strikes,
That my troubles are nothing compared to hers or his,
But I'm tired of telling myself that the answer to
Why does this happen to me is
Just lucky I guess.

IF ONLY

If only shopping at Saks counted as exercise.
If only aggravation made me thin.
If only there was a pill I could take for grace
    under pressure and upper-arm definition.
If only I lost as adorably as I win.

If only having insomnia gave me courage.
If only eating chocolate made me smart.
If only there was a cloth that washed off lipstick,
    mascara, eyeliner, blusher, and wrinkles.
If only my breasts and my waist were farther apart.

If only going to movies lowered cholesterol.
If only constipation made me rich.
If only there was a shot that would immunize me
    against impatience and feeling guilty.
If only I laughed as easily as I bitch.

If only French fried potatoes helped me remember.
If only they sometimes also helped me forget.
If only one morning I'd leap out of bed feeling ready
    and willing and eager to welcome old age.
But not yet.
Not yet.
Not yet.
But not quite yet.

ML   7/0